# Bricks

Edited by Rebecca Stefoff

Text © 1990 by Garrett Educational Corporation
First Published in the United States in 1990 by Garrett Educational
Corporation, 130 E. 13th Street, Ada, Ok 74820

First Published 1988 by A&C Black (Publishers) Limited, London with
the title BRICKS © 1988 A&C Black (Publishers) Ltd.

Manufactured in the United States of America.

**Library of Congress Cataloging-in-Publication Data**

Cash, Terry.
    Bricks / Terry Cash ; photographs by Ed Barber.
    p.   cm. - (Threads)
    Includes index.
    Summary: Explains how bricks are made and used in construction.
    ISBN 0-944483-68-2
    1. Bricks-Juvenile literature. 2. Brickmaking-Juvenile literature.
[1. Bricks. 2. Brickmaking.] I. Barber, Ed., ill. II. Title. III. Series.
TP828.C37        1990
666'.737-dc20                                        90-40249
                                                           CIP
                                                           AC

# Bricks

Terry Cash

**Photographs by Ed Barber**

### Contents

GEC **GARRETT EDUCATIONAL CORPORATION**

# Patterns in brick

How many buildings in your area are made of bricks? Have you ever wondered where so many bricks come from and how they are made?

Look at some walls and see the different patterns that the bricks make. Can you find some patterns like this ...

or this ...

or this?

If you have some toy bricks, try to copy some of these patterns. Build other walls using different patterns of your own. Can you think of a way of testing the strength of your walls?

3

# Looking at bricks

You could make a collection of different types of bricks.
You will probably need to ask an adult to help you.
Builders' supply stores sell many different kinds of bricks,
and a salesperson may let you have some broken pieces.

Don't go onto building sites to look for bricks; it is
dangerous. If you ask the supervisor, he or she may find
some spare bricks for you.

As well as real bricks, you can collect pictures of brick
buildings from magazines or newspapers.

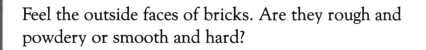

Feel the outside faces of bricks. Are they rough and powdery or smooth and hard?

Are all bricks the same reddish-brown color? How many different colors can you find?

Look at the bricks with a magnifying glass. Can you see black specks in some of them? Some bricks have pieces of burned coal in them.

What shapes are the bricks in your collection? Some bricks have holes through the middle. Other bricks have a dip in one side.

When building a wall, the bricklayer sticks the bricks together with a mixture of sand, cement, and water. This is called mortar. A brick with a dip in the top holds more mortar than a brick with a flat top. The extra mortar helps to hold the bricks together.

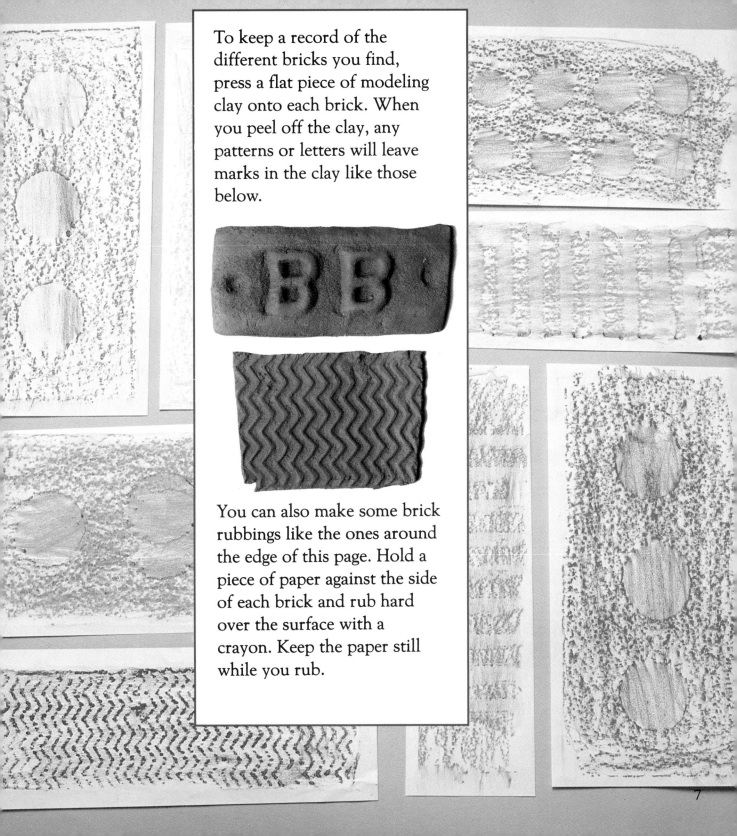

To keep a record of the different bricks you find, press a flat piece of modeling clay onto each brick. When you peel off the clay, any patterns or letters will leave marks in the clay like those below.

You can also make some brick rubbings like the ones around the edge of this page. Hold a piece of paper against the side of each brick and rub hard over the surface with a crayon. Keep the paper still while you rub.

# Measuring bricks

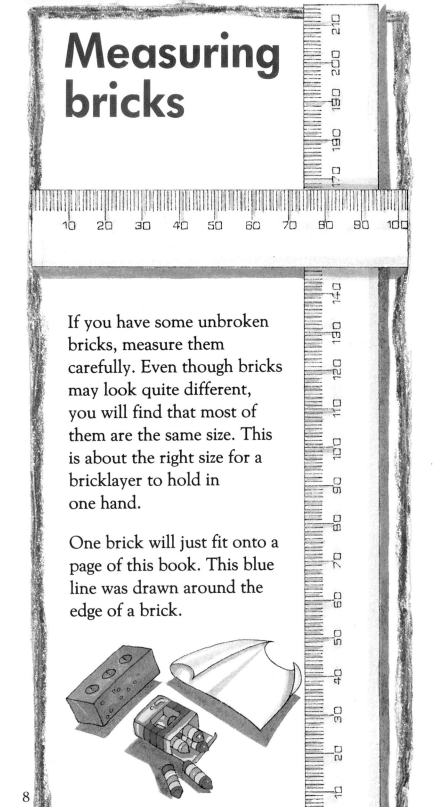

If you have some unbroken bricks, measure them carefully. Even though bricks may look quite different, you will find that most of them are the same size. This is about the right size for a bricklayer to hold in one hand.

One brick will just fit onto a page of this book. This blue line was drawn around the edge of a brick.

Can you guess how many bricks you would need to build a wall one yard high by one yard long? (This is called a square yard.)

Measure the outline of a square yard on a brick wall and count how many bricks are inside the square. Remember that two half bricks make one whole one.

# From soft clay to hard brick

Look at a brick at the very bottom of a tall building. How many bricks are piled on top of it? Bricks must be very strong to hold so much weight.

Most bricks are made from clay, which is dug out of the ground. Clay from the ground is soft and can be easily squashed in your hands.

What do you think makes soft clay turn into hard brick?

If you have a kiln at school, you will probably know the answer. A kiln is a special oven that bakes things at very high temperatures. This baking is called firing.

The inside of a kiln gets four times hotter than the hottest setting of an oven for cooking food. This heat drives the water out of the clay and makes it get hard, like stone. If a fired brick gets wet, it won't turn back into soft clay again.

9

# How to make bricks

Thousands of years ago, when the first bricks were made, kilns had not yet been invented. Bricks were made of mud that was baked by the heat of the sun. Straw was sometimes mixed with the mud to help bind it together and make the bricks stronger. In some hot countries, bricks are still made like this.

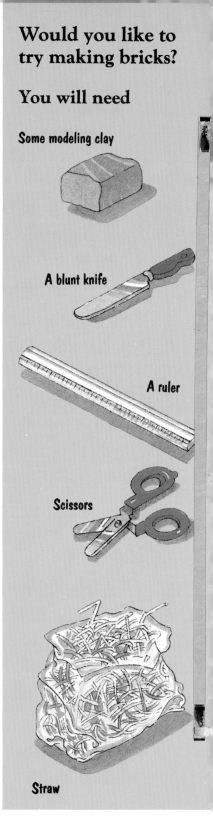

**Would you like to try making bricks?**

**You will need**

Some modeling clay

A blunt knife

A ruler

Scissors

Straw

1. Use the knife to cut the clay into small blocks. Make each block about 2 inches (4cm) long, 1 inch (2cm) wide, and 1/2 (1cm) inch deep.

2. Use the scissors to cut up some straw into very small pieces.

3. Mix the straw with some clay, and then cut some more bricks from the mixture of clay and straw. Make the bricks the same size as before.

Put all the bricks in a warm place to dry. When the clay is hard, the bricks are ready to use. Compare the clay and straw bricks with the plain clay bricks. Which bricks are stronger?

11

# In the factory

Today, most bricks are made in factories called brickyards. A big machine digs the clay out of the ground.

The clay is left in a huge pile next to the factory. For several months, the wind, rain, and frost break up the clay into smaller lumps. This makes the clay easier to shape into bricks.

Before the clay is shaped and fired, it is sometimes mixed with other materials, such as sand and coal. The coal will help the bricks to burn when they are fired in the kiln. Did you see any pieces of burned coal in the bricks you collected?

Inside the factory, a machine crushes the clay and mixes it with water to make a thick, sticky paste. If the clay is very wet, there may be no need to add more water to the mix.

# Making bricks by hand

These bricks are being made in molds.

**1.** First the wet clay from the crushing machine is squeezed and pressed to push out the air. Then the clay is rolled in some sand.

**2.** A wooden mold is also sprinkled with sand. The sand stops the clay from sticking to the mold. The mold is put on top of a metal block, which is fixed to the bench. The block is called a stock. The stock has a bump in the middle to make the dip in the brick. There are also some raised letters on top of the bump. These are the initials of the brickyard.

Mold

Stock

14

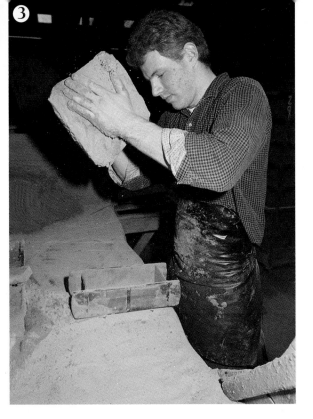

**3.** The clay is thrown down into the mold to press the dip and the letters into the clay.

**4.** Any extra clay is scraped off the top of the mold and used to make more bricks.

**5.** The mold is immediately lifted off the stock and the brick is tipped out onto a board.

It takes about one minute to make a brick by hand, and every handmade brick is different in some small way.

Bricks that are a special shape often have to be made by hand. They are more expensive than ordinary bricks. A new mold has to be made for each new shape.

How many different shapes can you see in the big photograph? Look for these special shapes near your home or school.

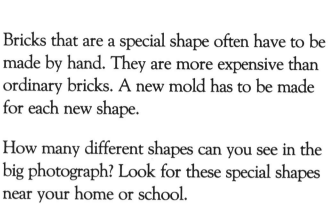

# Making bricks with machines

Machines can also make bricks in molds. This is much quicker and cheaper than molding bricks by hand. A machine can make thousands of bricks every hour. Can you figure out how many bricks a person can make by hand in one hour?

The other way of making a brick shape is for a machine to push the damp clay through a hole which is the same shape as the sides of a brick. This makes a long bar of clay.

Bar of clay

Bricks

A row of wires is then pressed through the bar of clay to slice it into bricks. In the photograph, can you see the wires?

In stores, people sometimes use wire to slice small pieces of cheese off a big block. Have you seen this done in the stores near your home?

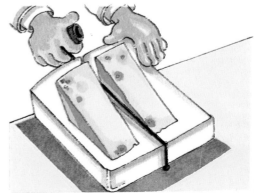

17

Most of the bricks that are cut with wires have holes through the middle. The holes are made by metal rods that are fixed in the brick-shaped hole through which the clay is pressed.

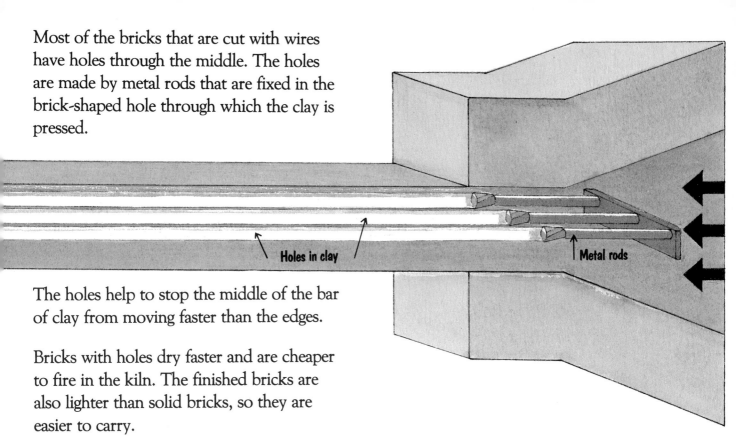

Holes in clay

Metal rods

The holes help to stop the middle of the bar of clay from moving faster than the edges.

Bricks with holes dry faster and are cheaper to fire in the kiln. The finished bricks are also lighter than solid bricks, so they are easier to carry.

Scraper

After the wet clay has been made into a brick shape, marks are sometimes made on the sides of the bricks. This can be done by hand or with a machine.

Sharp grains of sand, brushes, or scrapers are used to make the marks. You can try this yourself if you make some bricks.

# Drying the bricks

After the clay has been made into a brick shape, by hand or in a machine, it usually has to be dried before it is baked in a kiln. If the bricks are too wet, they may crack or crumble in the kiln.

The bricks are stacked on tall racks and left in a tunnel full of warm air for several days. As the bricks dry, they shrink a little.

When the bricks are dry, they are moved out of the tunnel and put into a kiln.

19

# In the kiln

This old-fashioned kiln is being loaded by hand. There are thousands of bricks to fit in, so it takes a long time.

The bricks have to be stacked with spaces in between them so that the heat can reach all the bricks—even those right in the middle. When the men have finished loading the kiln, it looks like this.

Brick kilns are heated by oil or gas. In this modern kiln, can you see the fire over the top of the bricks?

The bricks stay in the kiln for at least 24 hours. In a big kiln, the bricks may be baked for several days.

Look at this photograph. The brick at the back is ready to go into the kiln. The one in front has just come out of the kiln. What differences can you see?

When the bricks have cooled down, they are loaded onto trucks to be taken to builders' supply stores or building sites.

# Are bricks waterproof?

To keep buildings warm and dry on the inside, bricks must keep out the rain and damp. But are bricks waterproof? Try this test to find out for yourself.

## You will need

**A clean, dry brick**

**A bowl full of water**

**A cloth or paper towel**

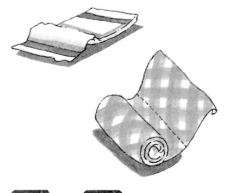

**Kitchen scales**

Weigh the dry brick and write down how much it weighs. Put the brick into the bowl of water and leave it there overnight.

Then use the cloth or paper towel to remove the water from the surface of the brick and weigh it again. The brick will be heavier because it will have soaked up some of the water like a sponge.

If bricks soak up water, buildings made of brick should be very damp inside. What can a builder do to stop this from happening?

Look carefully at the bricks at the bottom of a modern building. A few bricks up from the bottom, you should see a thicker line of mortar. You may be able to see the edge of a strip of black material in the middle of the mortar.

Damp-proof course

The black material goes right around the building. It is called a damp-proof course, or DPC for short. The DPC is made of thick, tarry felt or tough plastic. These materials are waterproof. They stop the water from getting through to the bricks above the DPC. Older buildings usually do not have a DPC like this.

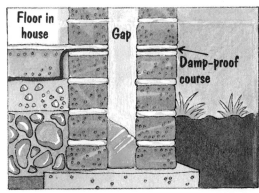

Floor in house
Gap
Damp-proof course

# Building with bricks

Now you know how a soft piece of clay from the ground can be turned into a hard, strong building material that lasts for hundreds of years.

Bricks can be used in many different ways.

**Factories**

**Bridges**

**Pavements**

**Chimneys**

**Houses**

**Tunnels**

**Walls**

**Schools**

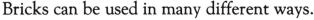

Bricks come in many colors and shapes, and they can be arranged to make lots of different patterns. Many people like the look of brick buildings. They think they are more interesting than building made of other materials, such as concrete. What do you think?

# More things to do

**1.** Did you make some clay bricks? (See page 10.) If your school has a kiln, perhaps your teacher will fire some of your bricks. Compare the difference between dried clay and fired clay. Try digging your thumbnail into a dried clay brick. Can you scratch the surface? Now try the fired brick. Does it feel the same?

**2.** How much space does a brick take up? Put a container inside a large bowl and fill the container to the brim with water. Carefully lower a brick into the container; make sure the whole brick goes under the water. Some of the water from the container will spill over into the bowl. This water takes up the same space as the brick. If you measure the volume of the spilled water with a measuring jar, it should be about the same volume as the brick.

**3.** Try making a damp-proof course. **You will need: 4** clean, dry bricks; 2 bowls; kitchen scales; a piece of DPC material or a thick plastic bag. **How to do it:** Put one brick into a bowl with the flat side upwards. Pour in enough water to come half way up the brick. Then weigh another brick and put it (flat side down) on top of the first brick. Do the same thing with the other bowl and the other two bricks. But this time, before you put on the second brick, lay the DPC or plastic bag across the top of the first brick. Leave the bowls for several days and watch how the water soaks up through the bricks. Then weigh the top bricks again. Has their weight changed at all? Has your damp-proof course worked?

**4.** If you tap a fired brick with the handle of a metal spoon, the brick will make a clear, chinking sound. But you may find some bricks that give only a dull thud when you tap them. These are called calcium silicate bricks. They are made from a mixture of sand, lime powder, and water. The mixture is like concrete and it is pressed into molds to make brick shapes. Calcium silicate bricks are not fired in kiln. Instead, they are steamed for several hours inside giant pressure cookers until they are hard and strong.

# Index